Pony Pointers

How to Safely Care for Your Horse or Pony

by Kathy Bennett
& Carol A. Peterson

This book is dedicated to mom and dad. Thank you for our first pony many years ago, our lives have been enriched by your encouragement and support.

All Rights Reserved: No part of this publication may be reproduced or transmitted in any form or by any means, electronic or mechanical, including photocopying, recording, storage in an information retrieval system, or otherwise, without the prior written permission of the publisher.

Limitation of Liability: In no event shall the publisher or the Author be held responsible nor liable for any indirect, direct, incidental, special, or consequential damages or costs whatsoever resulting from or related to the use or misuse of Pony Pointers even if the Publisher or the Author has been advised, knows, or should be aware of the possibility of such damages.

Any equine activity assumes an inherent risk.

published by Trail Trotters Book Ranch, Mason, MI
©2002 Carol A. Peterson
all rights reserved

Printed in the United States of America
by Dickinson Press Inc, Grand Rapids, MI

ponypointers.com

ISBN 0-9763209-0-8

If you want to ride horses and ponies, here are some pointers to help you get started . . .

Hi there, my name is Patchy and I am a pony because when full grown I'm under fifty-eight inches high at the withers (some breeds of ponies can only be fifty-six inches high). The main difference between a horse and pony, is size. Everything you learn about taking care of a pony, you can use with a horse.

Horses and ponies are the same in a lot of ways. We are all herd animals that group together as close friends. In a herd, we feel safe. We depend on each other to watch for anything that might hurt us. Because of this, we can be easily frightened by new or strange things.

Every herd has a leader. The lead pony is the first in line for food and water and is respected by the others. The leader is important because it keeps the herd organized in case of trouble or danger.

If we learn to trust you, we will think of you as our leader and respect you.

It is scarey to go to a new home, away from our old friends and the places we knew.

Some ponies need more time than others to get used to new things. But, once we feel safe, we will settle down and let you get to know us. A well-trained pony understands horsemanship and will be safe to handle; an untrained pony can be frustrating and dangerous. Once we get to know each other, if you feel I'm not right for you, it's okay to choose another pony that is a better match for your own personality and experience.

Many diseases and sickness can be avoided if the stall is kept clean.

Please don't tie me out on ropes or chains. Long ropes are dangerous. I could get my legs tangled up and break them, or get serious rope burns. I will be much safer and happier in a good fence or stall.

A balanced diet and proper exercise will keep me in healthy condition.

It is your responsibility not to let me get too fat...

or too thin!

A healthy diet includes mostly hay or grass, and a little bit of grain. Treats taste good, but too many are not good for me, and can make me sick.

A sick pony is uncomfortable and may lay down and get up several times in a row, or get sweaty and kick or bite at their sides. If I get sick like that, you should keep me walking and call a veterinarian (animal doctor). Your veternarian will decide if I have 'colic' and will help you make decisions about my care. Colic is a very serious condition and requires immediate medical attention.

Another problem caused by too much grain or treats is called founder, which causes permanent damage to the hooves.

The veterinarian is there to help you and will answer any questions you have about my health, care, and vaccinations. A healthy, well-cared for pony could live 20 years or more so when choosing a pony, don't overlook an older, gentle, well-trained pony.

Another important person is the farrier (blacksmith). My hooves grow continuously, just like your fingernails do, and about every six to eight weeks, the farrier should trim and balance them.

EXAMPLE OF GOOD HOOF

TOO LONG

SPLIT + CRACKED

VERY STEEP

Balanced hooves help my legs stay in good working condition. If the hooves get too long or if they are out of balance, it puts pressure and stress on my joints and ligaments and may cause pain and lameness. You cannot ride a lame pony that is in pain.

Hoof care is a part of each grooming session. The hoof should be cleaned with a hoof pick and checked for foreign objects, like stones. Hooves can also become dry and cracked and need hoof oil to moisten them.

Grooming is relaxing. Brush me often.

Begin with the rubber curry. It's great for that caked on mud; but don't use it on my legs or face, these places are too sensitive.

Next, use the stiff bristle body brush over my whole body, to lift the dirt off my skin.

Then, finish with a soft bristle brush to wisp away the dirt and bring out the shine of my coat.

Comb my tail by pulling it toward the side. Don't stand directly in front, or behind me, while grooming.

RUBBER CURRY

BODY BRUSH

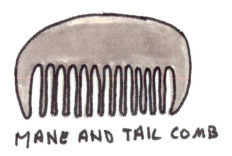

MANE AND TAIL COMB

HOOF PICK

Parts of the Pony

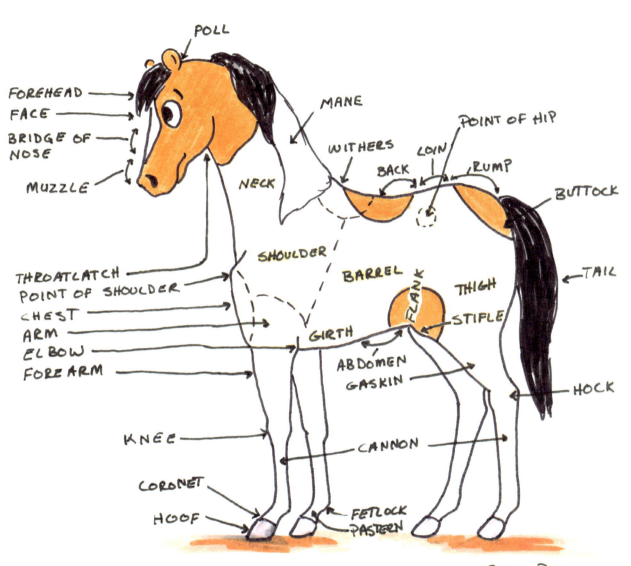

Please don't run up behind me. I kick to defend myself. When I'm scared or surprised, I kick. It's a pony reaction, so expect it and do not, I repeat, never ever run up behind me or any other horse or pony! Just don't do it!

If I get surprised or afraid, I might do anything to protect myself. Even if there is no real danger and the problem is just in my imagination. My natural instinct is to run or fight if I am scared.

Horses and ponies can be a lot of fun if you remember the safety rules.

Approach me in a calm and quiet manner from the side.

The halter is a piece of headgear that does not have a bit and it is used to control me from the ground. To put the halter on, don't push it onto my nose from the bottom, but gently pull it over my head from the top with your hand by my ears.

The lead rope is snapped to the bottom ring under my muzzle.

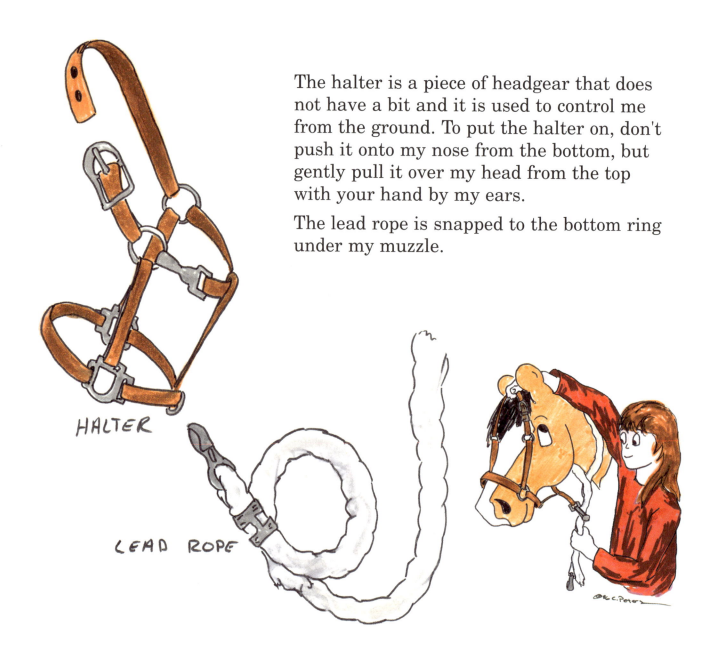

Stay out of the most dangerous places, which are directly in front or directly behind me, or sitting on the ground close to me. These are places where you could be stepped on, trampled, or kicked. And don't stand between me and a solid object, like a wall or fence, where you can't escape and might be crushed if I push against you.

Lead me from off to the side, near my head, where you can use the halter for control. Hold the lead rope with one hand below the snap, and the other hand around the outside of the extra rope and never, ever, coil the lead rope around your hand! If I get spooked and take off and your hand is tangled in a coil of the lead rope, I could drag you all over.

If I trust and respect you, I will be happy to follow you wherever you lead me.

My body will follow my head wherever it goes and my head is controlled by the halter. If you walk too far away from the halter, then I am in control and I will be leading you. Hmm, I wonder where I'd like to go . . .

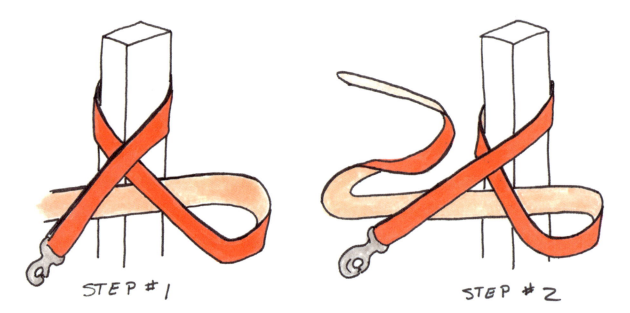

Safety knots are important because they can be quickly released by pulling on the hanging end of the lead rope. A pony should always be watched when tied

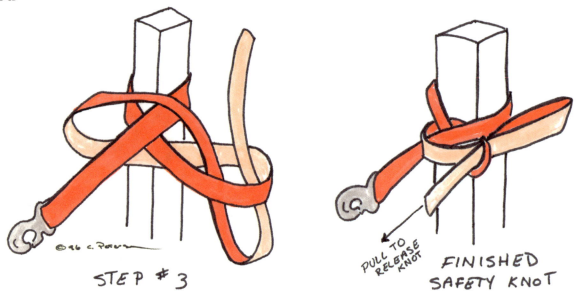

Tie me to a solid and secure object that cannot be pulled down or dragged.

Horse trailers can be scarey places for ponies because the space seems small and from the pony's point of view, there isn't a way to escape from danger. It takes time to teach a pony that trailers are okay places to be.

Here are some things to remember about trailering. Be patient. Don't try to rush me into a trailer. Don't trap yourself in the same area that you are loading me. Good trailers have escape doors and other places to stand when loading a pony.

Trailer ties have panic snaps on them. Panic snaps can be released with one simple pull on the spring.

Once a pony understands that trailers are okay, it will be easier and easier to get one in there. If you have a lot of problems with trailering, seek professional help.

One of my main concerns is to be comfortable. If any peice of my equipment is pinching, poking, and sliding all over, then I won't concentrate on what you ask me to do.

Horse size equipment is too big for a pony.

Riders need equipment, too. Cowboy boots and a helmet are essential. Cowboy boots have a solid heel that will help to prevent your foot from sliding through the stirrup and a properly secured helmet that meets safety standards will protect your head if you fall.

Parts of the Western Bridle

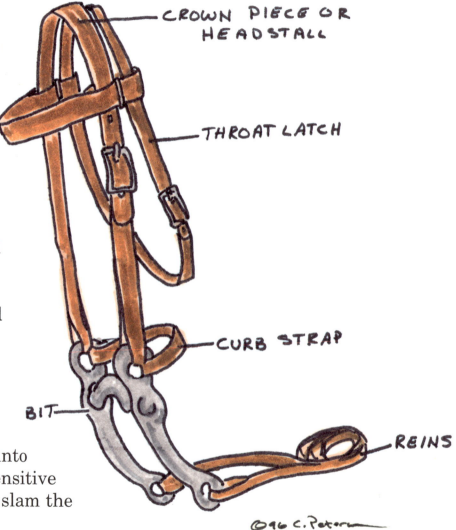

The bit of the western bridle should fit comfortably at the corners of my lips and be the same width as my mouth. If the bit is too wide, it will slide across my mouth. If it is too narrow, it will pinch. If the bit is uncomfortable, I'll think about it, instead of listening to your directions.

Pull the bridle over my ears from the top and use your other hand to guide the bit into my mouth. I have a sensitive mouth so please don't slam the bit into my teeth.

The reins are like a phone line that you use to talk to me. When you pick up the reins you are saying hello and I'm listening to you. I trust you to talk nicely to me through the reins and to protect my sensitive mouth from pain or injury.

Stepping on the reins can be frightening and painful and can make me nervous about the feel of the bit in my mouth.

Parts of the Western Saddle

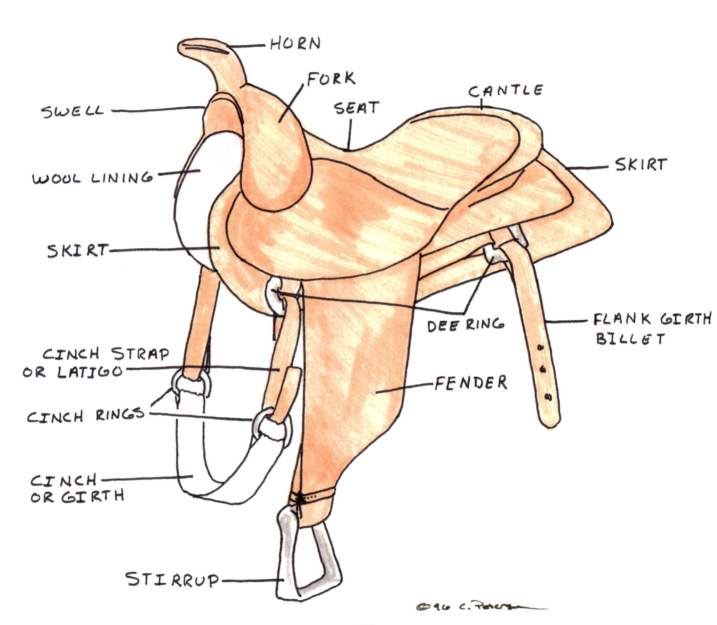

The front cinch is used to secure the saddle firmly to my body. Check the straps to be sure they are all flat and not twisted or pinching me.

The position of the cinch rings is above my elbow joints. If the rings are not above my elbow joint, I will bump into them every time my front leg moves.

Twisted, pinching straps and bumping cinch rings can cause bucking.

How to Tie a Western Saddle Knot

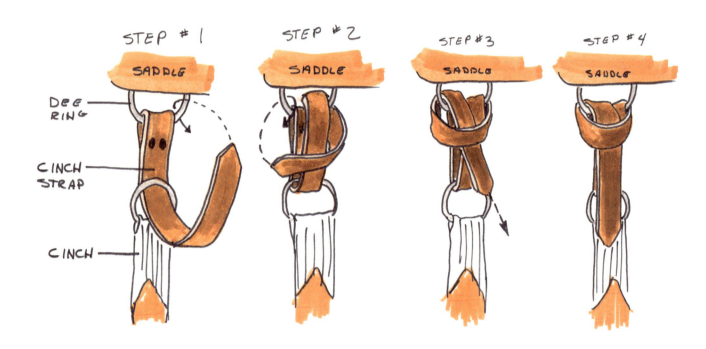

When you are securing the western saddle be gentle, I can be sensitive to the feel of the cinch tightening around me. You may need to tighten the cinch more than once before the saddle is safe enough for you to ride.

It is very important that the saddle is tight and secure. If the saddle slips...you could fall.

Nobody is perfect and there might be times when we don't understand each other. When that happens, remain calm and just try again.

Older, well-trained ponies are more experienced at figuring things out than the younger ones and can be less frustrating to ride. And safer, too!

Horsemanship means that you are able to control my direction and speed. I am trained to feel your legs and the reins, and to move away from pressure. The reins are used to tell me which direction to go and when to stop. I listen best when you have calm and gentle hands.

Reins that jiggle and bump the bit in my mouth are painful and I don't like it.

Leg pressure and rein pressure work together. Use only as much pressure as you need to get a response. I'm very sensitive to anything that touches me and it doesn't take a lot for me to feel what you are asking. I will move away from leg pressure and turn in the direction you push me toward, but sometimes it takes a lot of practice to get it right. Keep trying!

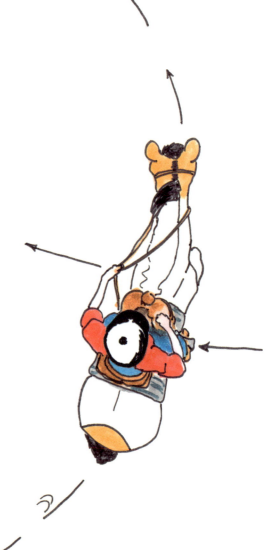

A relaxed, well-trained pony and a calm, gentle rider makes a nice team.

Pressure and release from pressure work together to tell me what to do, and if I did it right. My reward for moving away from pressure is that you stop pushing me.

When you pull the reins back, pressure on the bit tells me to stop going forward.

My reward for stopping is a release from pressure. So when I stop, remember to stop pulling on the reins or I might back up until you do.

The more you practice and get advice from experienced and professional horse people, the better you will understand good, safe horsemanship.